Touchea

Touched

a collection of erotic poetry
DUANE C. SCOTT

American Literary Press, Inc.
Baltimore, Maryland

Touched

Copyright © 2002 Duane C. Scott

Library of Congress
Cataloging in Publication Data
ISBN 1-56167-577-6

Other poems by Duane C. Scott appear in
Time After Time and *In-between Days*
published by the International Library of Poetry

Published by

American Literary Press, Inc.
8019 Belair Road, Suite 10
Baltimore, Maryland 21236

Manufactured in the United States of America

Dedicated to:

The nameless wonderful sweet as honey thing who inspired all things lovely being painted on the page of life. She knows who she is.

AUTHOR'S NOTES

Life is filled with expectations and is sometimes met with triumph and disappointment. However, there is a constant through all the turmoil of life. The ever-present companion to life is love. It is there when our children are conceived; it is there when our children come into this universal phenomenon called life.

Love is all around us. It is in the air we breathe, the water we drink, and the food we eat that is prepared by someone's loving hands. Love dances on the flame of a romantic candle and swims in every glass of white zinfandel wine. It is the consummate matchmaker. Love brings families together and can sometimes tear them apart. A very strange thing love. It is my shield from all the noise, from all the things that would like to imprison love.

Love is the true essence why these poems were written. I just hope that you, the reader, will enjoy reading them as much as I enjoyed writing them. Take them into the bubble bath or to the park or even in front of the fireplace and watch love blossom into something you won't be able to control between you and that special someone.

Love is and will always be what you will do with it.

UNTITLED

I slept in the nude last night
in hoping that you would appear in my dreams
wearing nothing but me.

2

I MISS YOU

I sit in my room and I rock with despair in hoping that the rocking will rock the pain of missing you away. I rock and rock but the motion seems to only make my pain worse.

I miss your smile, I miss your face, I miss your smell, and I miss your taste.

How can I go on this way, the tears keeping rolling and I'm blinded into oblivion where there is nothing but a sea of constant pain. I miss you and I can't function without thinking of you.

I miss your love, I miss your laughter, I miss your touch, and I miss your lips.

I walk and talk to myself. I lose my mind when you're not here. I hug myself hoping that you will suddenly appear within my arms. I hope against hope that I will never be without you again.

I miss your skin, I miss your toes, I miss your breath, I miss your heart, and I miss your sex.

I know I am crazy because I hear seagulls and I see you walking on the beach like you are an angel appearing from the heavens. I beg you to take me from my misery. Take me to the place where joy abounds in your arms.

I miss your eyes, I miss your voice, I miss your ears, and I miss **YOU!**

A LOVE POEM FROM THE MOST HIGH

Today I thought of you from beginning to end. Today I feel that life is worth living just because you live inside of me. Today I am on my way to heaven and heaven resides within you. Today is the day that I will be baptized by your loving tears. Today I will kneel and give thanks to the lord above for saving my life and the gift that he has given me, which is everlasting you. Today is the day that I say thank you for you.

Tomorrow is the day, that I will be a brand new me. One who is loved by the very grace of you. The grace that lifts me up when I am low; the grace that brightens my day when it is dark and gloomy; the grace humbles me when I get too high on self; the grace that dries my tears and dusts off my heart when it is broken. Tomorrow is the day that I will be a brand new me. Tomorrow I will rise and pray the prayer of thanks to you for washing me in the blood of grace. Tomorrow is the day of pure love, the love that you give me. Tomorrow is the day when the birds will sing a new song and the wind will dance a new dance and my heart will praise the day that I met you. Tomorrow is the day that I will be a brand new me thanks to you.

Forever I will cherish you as if it were my last days. I will kiss the sky in bliss for the blessings that rain upon me. You shower me with love and I know I am not worthy. Forever I will love you. Forever I will serve you. Forever I will be the mouthpiece that spreads your wisdom and compassion. Forever I will be in you. Forever is the day I met you.

UNTITLED

I have tasted bitterness ... I have savored
sweetness ... I have felt excruciating pain ...
I have felt pleasure divine ... I have known
hardship and heartache I have basked in
the realm of success and love... I have been
wronged and betrayed by others... I
know a God that is there to the end... I have
flirted with the certainty of death and I
relish the uncertainty of life but none can
compare with the emotional high, the
lovable, kissable, hugable, sexable life I share
with you.

ABUNDANT
LIFE
CELEBRATION
OF
BEAUTY
KINDNESS
INTELLIGENCE
SISTER
LOVER
FRIEND
WIFE
AND
YOU

STAY
WITH
THE
INFINITE
ABUNDANT
LOVE
ME

Intermingled sweat
between a man and a woman
is nature's sweetest potion when mixed with
love and sex.

"Bon appetite"

THE DEEPEST DARKEST SECRET

The relationship we have is forbidden and stolen. When I look into your windows that open to your soul I see a deep dark desire that is revealed only to me.

Hush you say, this is our deepest darkest secret that thing and place that only we occupy. Your whispers are soft as that of the breast of a dove. Touch me you say, taste me you plead, feel me you beckon, love me you demand, as one who demands righteousness in an unjust world.

I say this deepest darkest secret is ours to cherish forever lest we lose our lives. Life is passion, life is pain, life is desire pleasurable and fulfilling. Our secret our burden we must control it, or does the secret control.

Pay tribute to that thing which is beyond us? Never you say. Control is foreign to us yet the deepest darkest secret we share is ours to control. Your lips form the shape of seduction and kiss my apprehension away. It flies an endless flight never to return as long as I am in the company of your perfection.

At that instant you smile and it radiates warmth on a cold winter's day. Flesh to flesh, heart to heart beating as one, coming as one, one life, one love, and one secret, deep and dark.

GOD! I LOVES THAT WOMAN

God! I loves that woman.
I lose all control of my
senses and all reason when
she is near me.

She need not touch me,
Just her gaze upon me
and I will always riiise to the
Occasion.

God! I loves that woman. she puts
me in a trance under a spell, she
works her magic her voodoo. she is
definitely a voodoo woman
If you believe in that sort of thing,
Damn, I do.

God! I loves that woman.
I've lost weight, my mind,
and all sense of direction.
Yet, I've gained the sexual
Appetite of a rhinoceros in heat.
That is a good thing I think,

God! I loves that woman.
Her cat speaks to me in tongues
and my penis dances the dance
of forbidden seduction.

Her body wet, her body pungent with the
fragrance of pure honey and the elixir of sweet sex.
Her body sings to me. That urge to do, that urge to suck,
Lick; inhale her sweet femininity the very essence of self.
God! I loves that woman.

PERFECTION

Perfection, perfect in every way, not in the sense of pure perfection or the comparison of God like perfection; no, you are not omnipotent but you are perfect in my eyes.

You possess the kind of perfection that makes me laugh, makes me cry, and makes me smile. Your perfection is the kind that gives me life.

Perfection fleeting, perfection free, perfection captive, captivating me. Your perfection makes me hostage, your slave, my thoughts are of your perfection. Your perfect smile, that smile that radiates through to my bones.

You are as perfect as the spring morning dew. You sit there in your perfect way reflecting all light, all love, all peace, all perfection.

Do I dare covet a creature so perfect. Do I dare touch the hem of your garment. Do I dare fantasize about a frame so perfect. A frame so perfect that the Goddess Venus would be envious.

When I gaze upon your being I touch with my mind your breast, thighs and buttocks. I caress with with my mind and I make love to your infinite body. I do not mean to offend you I just want to make clear how your perfection has imprisoned me. I am a prisoner of your eyes and they pierce to my soul. I am a prisoner of your flawless smile as it warms my heart. I am a prisoner of your laughter as it tickles my funny bone. I am a prisoner of your voice as it communicates your perfection to me.

Am I lost in your perfection, am I adrift on a vessel that is surrounded by your perfection. Do I thirst for your perfect passion, do I hunger for your infinite joy, do I ache for your body with the longing of ten thousand men? Yes, yes, yes... Your perfection is boundless in a sea of dreams and in that sea there is me; just me and your perfection. You speak to me softly as only of one who is perfect. You tell me perfect dreams perfect tales and perfect loveliness that expends all my energy.

The sweet nectar of sweat and steam. The feel of pure perfected serenity with you and me naked to the world but seen by none. Your perfection, your sweetness, your love and perfection me.

PHOENIX

Rising from the ashes, new birth, new life, new faith. The emptiness inside was replaced with a wholeness not realized, with a warmth not felt before, like a PHOENIX rising from the ashes, you have given me new life.

Life not known, fire not felt, the flame cool and frigid, the melting of ice and snow, the desolation of life renewed and propagated. Your warmth, your smile like the PHOENIX rising from the ashes you have given me birth.

Music sweet and low, water warm and toasty, lights dim and restful, your love is blessed and sweet. I am naked to the world but I am revealed only to you. My spirit is exposed and vulnerable, my life is in a precarious state, but like the PHOENIX I am rising from the ashes propped by your flaming appendages I am loved and cared for.

The PHOENIX is my constant companion she is always there and not there, she is part of me and not part of me, she is fun, she is free, she is love, she is me. PHOENIX, fly to me, fly with me, and stay with me. Rising from the ashes, new life, new love, new birth, PHOENIX my life, my love, my friend.

POEM FOR C.

How does a man continue to love someone on a day in day out basis without becoming redundant? How does he start a new day with all it has to offer that is fresh and new and know that the love he carries for a certain woman will be the same? How is it possible to wake up in the middle of the night and know that the dream he has of that woman is always new always refreshing and exhilarating? If you knew C. you would know.

How is it feasible to touch a woman a million times and still with every touch have your breath taken away. How is it scientifically possible to kiss the back of her neck and have thoughts run wild about her wonderful feet? Why is it that this woman keeps me on a path of pure ecstasy and she is not even physically with me. If you knew C. you could see why.

How is it possible to make love to a woman and never get tired or even lose any desire to please her over and over again? How is it possible to kiss her body and still discover something new about every pore, hair, crevice, or any part of her supple skin. There is some force that compels me to think- of her twenty-four hours a day and still the thoughts are as fresh as the first one that I ever had of her. Why in heaven's name can I look at her and start to want to cry tears of joy because she just smiles at me. If you knew C. than you would be able to relate.

How come, how come I can't get her out of my mind. Why is she haunting me every way I turn'? Yet the haunting is sweet surrender of my mind to her every whim. Why is it that her touch, the sound of her voice, the crack of her crooked smile or even the way she walks makes me weak at the knees? Why in the world do I have tunnel vision and at the end of that tunnel there she stands. If you knew C. well, I need not say anymore.

She is a dream wrapped up in an enigma and I am the only one to solve the riddle of the love I have for her with no time on the clock. She is all I want out of life. She is wealth, she is love, She is fertility, She is a child, she is stability and life all wrapped into a five foot two package of unparalleled beauty. 'Why ask why anymore. She is everything any man would want in a woman. She is perfection to me and the envy of the Gods. She is heaven here on earth she is my Garden of Eden. I need not say any more about C.

I must go on because I would be remiss in my duty because it would take a millennium to describe how I feel about this woman. There will never be enough stars in the sky to match the reasons why I love this woman. Why is it that the curves of her body make me lose control Why would I give my life for her? Why would I feel like I have to give her everything I have. Why, why, why.

She is me, She is me and I just don't know why I need her so. Her hair it grows a certain way that only I could enjoy. She is intelligent and Einstein could not hold a candle $E=Mc2$ to her scientifically perfect beauty. How come I wait in my car at a light and I see her in my rear view mirror? Why is it that while driving down the road every plant, bush, or tree reminds me of her. I do not have all the answers, just the facts and the facts say that I am a slave to her rhythm.

Put the ring in my nose and lead me anywhere you want, my mind says to her when I look upon her endless beauty. I buy flowers because they are just a small reminder of her sweet fragrance. Her bouquet should be patented and I should be the only one to hold all rights to the wealth of such a wonderful aroma. Why am I feeling this way? How come this happened to me? Am I the victim? These are questions that come up with only one answer I don't care, I am in love with this woman.

So you see the questions are irrelevant but the emotion is all-powerful as powerful as the love I have for C.

SUNSHINE

Sunshine with the sunny disposition. She is bright and fiery with the taste of pure honey.

Sunshine kisses all that she possesses, I just wished that I could kiss her. Her kiss would penetrate my very soul. Her sunshine would transform me into a sunburst bright and fleeting. For that fleeting moment my life is pure, radiant and free.

Sunshine smiles and the brilliance blinds me into her oblivious warmth. Sunshine with her golden color of softness and sheen; I wished that I could possess her.

Sunshine speaks to me in kindness, in love, in peace, and in laughter. I wish, I wish, I wish, that Sunshine was a part of me.

YOUR SMILE

Your smile is that very thing that I live for. I want to bask in its bright warm light. The sun would be a copy of a smile so bright. Your warmth and kindness emanates from your smile. Your smile is like a spring rain it is fresh and a source of life so divine. Your smile is contagious it spreads exuberance to everyone it touches. It touches me and my life is fulfilled.

Your smile is a sea of grins where laughter is the norm and sadness is fleeting. Your smile is where I want to be. It touches me in the morning and it adds meaning to a meaningless day. It adds light to a gloomy day. It adds sweet, sweet moisture to a parched soul. Your smile is living proof of excited ecstasy. I get lost in your smile and I don't want to ever be found. I want to dance to the rhythm of your laughter. Sway to the sexiness of your voice as it swings to the beat of pure happiness that is your smile.

Your smile is love is peace is serenity is kindness is sincerity is jovial is sweet is sexy and is the road home to my baby's touch. Your smile is everything to me. It inspires, tantalizes, energizes, is mythical, magical, and naughty and for that one fleeting moment when you smile, that smile belongs to me.

THE ORIGINS OF LUST

The origins of lust, a spark, a twinkle, a sudden glance, the rise of an, eyebrow.

The origins of lust it controls even the purest of moralists. The crack of a smile, a sudden stare, eyes fixed on breasts, crotch, behind, legs, feet, or hands.

The origins of lust, a touch, a brush, the blushness of lips, the sound of a voice, a laugh, a sigh.

The origins of lust, pulse quickens, heart labors, hands sweat, the liquid of excitement, the heat of the moment, the moment, the origins of love.

Repeat

STATEMENT

This is not a poem but a statement of fact. This is something a little different, it doesn't involve the stars or the moon or anything to do with our terrestrial universe. It doesn't involve anything of our celestial world or anything to do with the spiritual realm but it has everything to do with you.

The difference is that you are far removed from the rest of our surroundings. The rest of us just live our lives connected with our environment we are part of the circle of life so to speak. However, you are different, you are above the stars and more down to earth than the soil that the rest of us toil. You are more spiritual than the essence of all human life; you are the one that I worship. Not in the sense that I hold you in esteem above God but in the sense that nothing else matters when I'm with you.

Let me explain. When you're with me or talking to me or when I'm thinking of you everyday life seems to fade like that of dust trailing behind a car on a lonely dry highway. Only you can smile and its magic surround me, only you can hold me and give me the strength of a thousand men. Only you can make me fall in love, only you.

So you see this is a statement of fact. It is not a philosophy or some kind of religious belief. It is just a statement of fact. Just like the laws of physics or that 2 and 2 equals 4 or that the sun rises every morning or that the love I have for you is true, these truths are self-evident. They exist without the help of man or any physical force that can be comprehended. These are the facts and I have accepted them with vigor and I am your ready and willing servant who will do anything for you.

This statement is overwhelming I know but I could not hold it within me because this entity, this statement, would have consumed me if it were not let out for the world to see and you are my world.

OPEN WIDE

Open wide those legs girl and spread your pussy pate' all over my face ... open wide your mouth girl and guzzle the wine of my passion ... get on your knees girl and let your ass rise to my occasion ... your moans are like music to the symphony of sex ... open wide your eyes girl and see the long boat of desire ... open wide your mind girl and picture the lake of eroticism ... open wide girl just open wide.

I WANT

I want to take your coat and make you
comfortable
I want to run a hot shower and undress
you
I want to bathe you soothe you and make
you sweet
I want to rub you down with sweet oils lotions and edible
potions
I want to tantalize you with every probing touch of my
fingers
I want to lay you down
I want to gaze upon your beauty and soak your essence
into my ever expanding love
I want to taste you from toe to head my tongue hard and
supple dripping with the flavor of you
I want to give love, give pleasure, give sex, give pleasure
give pleasure, give love, give me
I want you to be, I want you to see, I want you to know,
I want you to feel, I want you to be for you and for me.

WORD ASSOCIATION

When I say love you say.   YOU!
When I say sex you say.   YOU!
When I say pleasure you say.   YOU!
When I say screams you say.   YOU!
When I say beauty you say.   YOU!
When I say power you say.   YOU!
When I say rare and exquisite you say. YOU!
When I say supple you say.   YOU!
When I say breath of life you say.   YOU!
When I say arousal you say.   YOU!
When I say heat you say.   YOU!
When I say you. You say.   ME!

If you are sleeping, if you are smiling, if you are naked and if you are with me than I MUST be dreaming.

FOREVER

I try to push myself away from the table but I am forever hungry. I try to stop filling my cup but I am forever thirsty. I try to stop thinking of making love to you but I am forever horny. I try to deny myself the pleasure of knowing you but I am forever yours.

FIRST KISS POEM

Sometimes my tongue gets tied
Some times the words I express
don't flow like that of a river and
sometimes I don't have the
abundance of thought like that of
a well brimming with water.

It is times like these where one
solitary action is enough to express
how I feel about you. So this one
singular kiss should be enough to
show you exactly how I feel about
YOU.

YOU MAKE ME HIGH

Breathe in those fumes... smell that fragrance... my head spins and my nature rises... you make me high.

Touch me anywhere... I don't care just touch me ... my pulse quickens my heart races my toes curl and my mouth waters ... you make me high.

Intoxicate me with your touch make me drunk on your kiss and make me munch on your...damn you make me high.

Spread your legs as wide as the earth and squeeze the life out of my body Make me high ... make me high ... make me high.

Uncontrollably I lick the spot I'm addicted to; see the track on my tongue ... make me high girl ... make me high.

My lips they are numbed by the body cocaine of you, from your head to your toes, my senses are on overdrive ... make me high.

My fingers will stimulate ... make me high... your breasts they will titillate............make me high ......your ass will scintillate...make me high and my...will cremate ... make me high ... make me high ... make me high ... please make me high.

I'm spent... I'm used ... you made me high... I rest for now ... you made me high ...you touch .....you kiss ....you make me high I rise I laugh I'm high ...I'm high... you make me high.

ENOUGH

There isn't enough water to quench the
thirst I have for you, there isn't enough
food to silence the hunger I have for you,
there isn't enough medicine to ease the
pain I have for you, there isn't enough
space in the world that I wouldn't give to
you, and there isn't enough stars in the sky
to wish upon so that I may be with you.

MY BLACK WOMAN

My Black Woman, My Black Woman you are strong and you are weak. My Black Woman you are beautiful and unique. You are like the lifeline of faith sent from heaven above, and you are the soldier of temptation sent from Lucifer, of which I have no defense.

My Black Woman your skin is as soft as the touch of a mink, and your heart is like gold, full of the wealth of love. You are a child of Mother Africa and her fragrance enhances your every being. The complexity of self further intrigues me. You are an enigma wrapped up in one gorgeous Nubian package. You are Ebony, You are Sandalwood, You are Burnt Sienna, and High Yellow Cream, but deep in the heart of your soul you are still Black to me.

My Black Woman, My Black Woman do not release me, hold me tight and squeeze the selfishness from me and breathe submission and devotion of love into me. I am hypnotized by your elegance, it draws all my energy and resources, I am powerless yet strong I am weak yet fortified, it is your personal voodoo that has me confused.

My Black Woman your smile is so bright like the sun penetrating my soul. It radiates heat, that heat of passion and arousal. My black woman you are everything to me yet everything that is forbidden. You are that forbidden fruit in my personal garden of Eden. I want to take a bite and taste your deliciousness. Mmmmmm, your taste is divine is sinful and decadent. Please may I have some more.

I will consume all of you and I will be consumed by you. You are an addiction of which I cannot get enough. I will sell my house my car my soul just to make you My Black Woman, That Black Woman, My Black Woman, You Black Woman.

THE BLUES

As I sit watching the oblivion of God's sky my eyes peer into the brightness of the sun's rays as they grab the clouds and move them out of the way, all I can think of is you.

The sun's color of orange and yellow and purple of late evening; as he holds onto the daylight like a swimmer holds his breath all I can think of is you.

The relentless stagnation of the cloud's stubbornness, of their immovable force, the density of their ice crystals, reminds me of the times that I am not with you.

The thought of knowing that the sun sets and he gives way to the mystery of night, the Goddess of darkness reminds me of how my heart feels when I am not with you.

Yet, I know that the sun will triumph with every morning and it gives me renewed strength. For I feel you in my thoughts and touch you in my mind.

The dawning of a new day brings the rise of you and the glory of love. So you see my blues are of a temporary nature because I know your sunshine will wash my blues away. Like the sun triumphs at the dawning of a new day.

SLEEP DEPRIVATION

It is my opinion that since I have known you my desperation for sleep at night has been replaced by the desperation for you.

BLACK HOLE

In the darkness of night I search for your black hole... it beckons me from afar... it whispers my name ... your black hole it sucks all will from me ... I am vacuumed into your black hole ... black hole, black hole, has me in a trance... I am weightless and floating to your black hole... it is moist and warm and wet and ohhh so delicious ... your black hole is where I want to be... where there is absence of light there lies new life within that black hole ... black hole sings, sings, sings out my name... I am a beast ready to devour your black hole... I hunger I thirst for the juice from your back hole, I need that black hole... your black hole my black soul matched together like black gold.

MAKING BREAKFAST

The smell of bacon and eggs and toast and juice, the replenishment from the night before but what that aroma really means is that you spent the night with me for the first time and now you're making breakfast.

FIRE WORKS

Succulent savvy that sizzles like eggs on the griddle, that's what you do to my soul. Seconds are like days and weeks are like years, that is what I hope it will be when I'm making love to you.

When you look at me your eyes pierce like arrows through my heart; its blood shedding only for you. They say that love can move mountains but my love for you can alter the cosmos. C'mon and let me show you how the stars revolve around you.

Close your eyes and let me take control of your mind body and soul and you watch the stars in your mind explode like fire works. Shit, this must be love.

You know I just can't help myself but that addictive urge that I have to taste you controls it's like crack ...wait a minute it is a crack that beckons me hither and I am a slave to its whisper. Spread, spread, spread those fudgesicles I call legs and let me show you the meaning of the 4th of July. Fire works never looked so bright.

LAST NIGHT

Last night I lay in my bed with only my thoughts of you. The sound of your voice haunting me of our last meeting.

Last night it was quiet, as I lay there naked with only the vision of your naked body next to mine. I sigh a sound that I know you would relish.

Last night was a sleepless night filled with deep guttural sounds of making love. The sounds of flesh and friction and slapping and lapping and relief but only in my dreams.

Last night I lay in my bed and I cried for you with an insatiable appetite, a craving to taste you, my stomach roared with pain, my heart burned with desire. I needed you, so last night will become tonight.

OUR THUNDERSTORM

Lightning flashes, thunder rolls, rain wet, bodies wet with sweat, the rain our lubricant. You and I 'in the rain making love as the rain makes love to us, your sighs are that of thunder and my thrusts are that of lightning, we create our own thunderstorm. The rain covers us in a veil of secrecy; others slumber unaware of the storm we create. Thunder, lightening, you, rain, coitus, and me. OUR THUNDERSTORM.

UNTITLED

I make my heart like stone it is a fortress
that must withstand the onslaught of
emotion. My life is made of steel cold and
hard but softens with your blue hot flame
of love. Why do you put me in pain, why
did I have to fall in love with you. My heart
turns to dust crushed by the sledge of love.
Now I am vulnerable and ready for that
broken heart which you will hang around my
neck as my badge of shame. The price to pay
for falling in love with you,

NOIR GRACE

Noir, meaning black, dark as the night. Some will say that black is the absence of light, they will even go as far as calling black the playground for evil. They have obviously not seen you. Noir full of grace the adornment of life. The opulence of your beauty enhances the world. Your skin is as soft as the breast of a dove but black as beauty, black as grace.

Your voice dances on the winds of life. It sings the body electric; it is the true music for all other rhythms are out of tune. Do you hear it... can you see the sounds of blackness beating in my heart ... there is no other sound like the decibels of your voice... the true voice of blackness.

Yes, I do agree black is beautiful, it does have light, the light of eternal mind. My mind belongs to you I will lavishly squander it for you. I've done it a thousand times yet you are unaware. Black light, black life, black grace, black you.

I've been there once, but my soul has been to your black grace a million times; time and again. Your light shines like a trillion stars yet you are unaware. You make my pulse quicken yet you are unaware. My eyes behold the jewels of your soul yet you are unaware. I've touched your body... I've tasted your humanity and again you are unaware. Black grace, Noir grace adorns my life.

DIRTY MIND

Thrusts of a locomotive... spinning of a drill... the hum of an electric motor ... the insertion of a needle ... jack hammers thumping ... whales exploding into the air during feeding time... SCREAMS ... SLAPPING SOUNDS ... luscious red lips (both sets) ... waves crashing between legs... steam escaping from a tea kettle... going into a tunnel... licking lips (both sets)... reggae music ... drums beating... my baby putting a bottle of whatever to her lips ... pool stick in between fingers.. sweat on my woman... ice cream cones, popsicles, watermelon, and summer heat ... women riding bicycles... those new exercise machines ... rockets taking off.. fire, heat smoke, you, me beds, and ... well, use your imagination.

IN BONDAGE

Your love is like bondage
I am a slave to your rhythm
I am bonded to your beauty
I am a captive to your sexuality
I have no will but service to your will
Your love is like bondage sweet bondage.

INTELLECTUAL LOVE POEM

WONDEROUS SELF

ARDOR

PRETENTIOUS YOU

PRISONER

Prisoner bound by chains, freedom
Lies before me, I will not escape
Your eyes, they bind me, your touch
Is sweet salvation, your kiss is the
Lock that keeps me in place,
I sink to my knees and beg for mercy,
the mercy of your bondage.
Your will
Your prisoner
For life.

PRISONER

FREEDOM
MY CRIME

YOUR LOVE
MY SENTENCE

UNTITLED

Say nothing... for you must listen to this... sweet redemption from my boorish behavior... one look at you and I am saved from myself.. your beauty purifies me... cleanses me ... washes me in the wrap of your embrace... I am dizzy with desire ... I swing like a pendulum from pain and despair to joy and love with every thought of you ... yesterday I was dark and full of nothingness... today I am bright and full of life with YOU.

CREATION

The clouds in the sky with their varied shapes and sizes
with luminous color
cannot match the luminous splendor of your soul.

The fire of the stars the twinkle of their light does not
compare to how you
brighten my life and inflame my being.

The blush of clear blue water and crisp mountain air
cannot compare to the
freshness of you.

Like early morning dew on the adolescence of life I wake
with your creation
on my mind praying that we will be able to create to-
gether.

DO YOU MIND

Do you mind if I talk dirty to you? C'mon girl all I want to do is penetrate your mind and ride down your highway of lust where my final destination will be the forest of planet pubic. Do you mind if I talk dirty to you?

I want to scintillate and titillate your soul climb upon your summit called your ass and claim my spot. I want you to ride me as if your life depended on every stroke. Do you mind if I talk dirty to you?

The protrusions called your breast so perfect as if they were holy ground I will put off thy clothes and pay tribute with my tongue. Your nipples erect and succulent oh how I worship their deity. C'mon girl let me talk dirty to you.

I don't mean to offend but I just want to lick your lips and I don't mean the sweet set on your lovely face I mean that sweet set calling my name from way down yonder. I want to smother myself in your sweetness gasping for air as you moan in ecstasy and oblivious to my plight. Do you mind if I talk dirty to you?

I want to spread you and perform surgery I want to administer anesthesia and put you out into a world filled with pleasure. C'mon girl let me talk dirty to you, hell fuck all that talking and let me show you how dirty I can be.

STILLNESS

be still like the still of the night
close your eyes and let the stars
paint your mind.

what do you feel what do you see
how does it taste and what do you
hear.

let me express my feelings as I stroll
into your playground of thought
i want to get inside your mind
i want to fill you up with every inch
and ounce of me.

we will never be separated we are
connected your thoughts my thoughts
your body my body you are me
and I am you.

DESIRE

Desire is what flames my soul. My soul shakes, it rattles and it rolls with desire that I have for Desire.

Her name is Desire, for she grips my blood and grabs my fiery mind and intoxicates me with desire. Her breasts and her deep dark sun drenched figure needs no drapery. For it is immaculate and she leaves me with desire.

My blood boils with desire for Desire. Her fragrance I sense in my slumber her thoughts become my thoughts, her mind my mind, her body my body, we are one and we are called desire.

I will sweat in the deep passionate thought of desire, she will tempt me, she will use me as she will, I am her slave and I am not ashamed for desire has taken my soul. I will not care, for desire is me and desire is Desire is you.

THE FOG

Vague is my mind
Intellect lost
Sense of direction displaced
By confusion
The state of my life without you.

BLESSED DREAMS

I had a dream about you last night
floating on the winds of sleep
where only I can possess you.

Your body perfectly sculpted
in sweet fleshy divinity
my hands performing
rhythmic pulsating massage
and it is I who floats away
on orgasmic peace.

Your body haunts me in
this peace thank god for
haunting dreams but it
is the devil that curses my
bliss with the dawning of
morning it seems.

HAIR, PORES, AND TOUCH

Warmth of skin across my face
the feeling of the tiny tantalizing hairs
no The filling of the pores with wetness
The taste of you beneath my mind.

Skin soft and succulent tasty and delectable
the tickle, the tingle, the heat of ecstasy
your breath heavy and laborious the sound of pleasure.

Touch me, touch you, we are pasted together no air between us
stolen together, steal my heart and my soul.
Images capturing my life with you and your essence
the touch of skin the stimulation of hairs and the filling of pores.

Writing for you is like having sex, every time the ink hits the paper I have an orgasm of brilliant proportions. My very best is once again expended, my heart, soul and love is all at once shot like a cannon and explodes all over the canvas known as paper. Although the paper is oblivious to my pleasure; it does perform the important function of delivering these orgasmic episodes to your hands, mind, body and soul so that you may experience the same ecstasy as I.

THE END GAME

There is no end
as long as
I am loving you.